The Story of
SACAJAWEA
Coloring Book

Peter F. Copeland

DOVER PUBLICATIONS, INC.
Mineola, New York

Bibliographical Note

The Story of Sacajawea is a new work, first published by Dover Publications, Inc., in 2002.

DOVER *Pictorial Archive* SERIES

This book belongs to the Dover Pictorial Archive Series. You may use the designs and illustrations for graphics and crafts applications, free and without special permission, provided that you include no more than four in the same publication or project. (For permission for additional use, please write to Permissions Department, Dover Publications, Inc., 31 East 2nd Street, Mineola, N.Y. 11501.)

However, republication or reproduction of any illustration by any other graphic service, whether it be in a book or in any other design resource, is strictly prohibited.

International Standard Book Number: 0-486-42374-3

Manufactured in the United States of America
Dover Publications, Inc., 31 East 2nd Street, Mineola, N.Y. 11501

To Anne Copeland Dorchies, my granddaughter

NOTE

Sacajawea's story was nearly forgotten for a hundred years, and was rediscovered through the work of researchers at the US Bureau of Indian Affairs. Today we know a great deal about this heroic Native American woman whose faithful service to the explorers of the Lewis and Clark expedition helped make their remarkable journey a success.

For a more detailed story of the Lewis and Clark expedition, see my *Lewis and Clark Expedition Coloring Book*, Dover Publications, 1983.

PETER COPELAND

1. Sacajawea, an Indian girl. Sacajawea was born in 1789, a daughter of a chief of the Shoshone people in the Rocky Mountains of present-day Idaho.

2.   **The call of the wild geese.** It is said that, as a girl, Sacajawea was fascinated with the call of the wild geese as they flew over the mountains on their way north in the spring. She longed to follow them on their journey.

3. Shoshone children at play. Life was good for the Shoshone people. Buffalo were plentiful; their meat supplied food and their hides were made into winter robes and moccasins. Antelope and deerhide were made into buckskin for clothing. Summer was a carefree time.

4. **Children's chores.** Shoshone children, both girls and boys, had chores to perform each day. Life was not all fun and games. Here we see young **Sacajawea** helping her mother prepare food for an evening **meal**.

5.   Fieldwork. Women and girls also worked in the fields tilling the garden crops the Shoshone planted every spring. Here Sacajawea helps her mother till the soil with a hoe made from buffalo bone.

6. Moving day. The Shoshone followed the migrating buffalo herds. When it was time to move, it was the job of the women and girls to pack the household goods.

Here we see Sacajawea and her mother packing their family's possessions, including teepee poles, onto a horse-drawn travois.

7. **Sacajawea and her brother.** Sacajawea idolized her older brother, who taught her many things which he himself **had** learned from his teachers and the other men of the tribe. He was learning the craft of the hunter and the duties and skills of the warrior, protector of his people.

8. **The education of Sacajawea.** Sacajawea learned many things from the old ladies of the tribe. She was shown the plants used for healing and making medicine. She was taught to find leaves that cured sores and boils, and roots that cured poisoning and snakebite.

9.   A visit to the tribal elders. The old men of the tribe passed on their knowledge and the history of their people to the village youth, so that tribal traditions and wisdom would continue. Here Sacajawea is brought by her mother to visit two elders who had long before traveled over the western mountains and seen the great lake of bitter waters that lay at the edge of the world—the Pacific Ocean.

10. Following the buffalo. Eveyone looked forward to the big buffalo hunt that occurred every fall. Hunting was the responsibility of the men. If the hunt was successful there would be a feast of fresh meat for everyone, with plenty left over to be dried for the lean winter months to come. The women would have much work preparing the meat and making the hides into winter clothing and sleeping robes.

11. The buffalo hunt. Buffalo hunts were conducted according to a traditional, carefully worked-out plan. The mounted hunters trapped the buffalo by quietly surrounding the grazing herd on three sides. Then, waving blankets and screaming, they would stampede the herd toward the open side, which led to a cliff over which the buffalo would be driven, to fall to their death in the valley below.

12.   The attack of the Hidatsa warriors. During one hunt, the Shoshone hunters were returning to their camp when they were suddenly attacked by a war party of their old enemy, the Hidatsa tribe. These warriors possessed guns (acquired by trade with white men) and quickly overcame the hunters, who were armed only with bows and arrows and lances.

13. **Sacajawea hides herself.** Soon the Hidatsa warriors, having overcome the hunters, found the Shoshone hunting camp. Sacajawea hid in the rocks beside a stream, hoping the warriors would not see her.

14. Taken by an enemy warrior. A Hidatsa warrior spotted Sacajawea and captured her. Her captor took her, with some other Shoshone captives and some stolen horses, on a long journey to the lands of the Hidatsa people on the Missouri River.

15. The Hidatsa village. The Hidatsa war party, with its captives and plunder, traveled for many days back to its village on the banks of the Missouri. Finally Sacajawea was brought to the lodge of her captor, Running Wolf.

16. Running Wolf's lodge. Running Wolf told Sacajawea that she must obey his commands and those of his wife, Grass Woman. Sacajawea was their slave.

17. **Sacajawea's life as a slave.** Sacajawea had to work hard, but was well treated. She and the other captive girls worked in the fields, carried heavy burdens, set up hunting camps, and loaded pack animals, all work that she had become accustomed to at home. She was young and strong and confident that one day she would somehow return to her people.

18. **The white man.** One day a white man named Toussaint Charbonneau came to the village. He told stories of the faraway places he had seen. Sacajawea listened with the others and was fascinated with his tales and with his strange appearance. He soon left, but appeared two days later at Running Wolf's lodge. Soon Running Wolf told Sacajawea that the white man had purchased her and that she must go with him. Sacajawea gathered her few belongings and followed Charbonneau to his camp.

19. Fort Mandan. Charbonneau took Sacajawea to a great log building like nothing she had ever seen before. This was Fort Mandan, on the upper Missouri River. There Charbonneau engaged other white men in talk that she could not understand. Later he told her that they would travel west with these men in the spring, toward the homeland of her people, the Shoshone. Sacajawea was happy to hear this.

These strange men were members of the Lewis and Clark expedition, which had been sent by President Thomas Jefferson to explore North America all the way to the Pacific Ocean. The expedition's leaders were Captain Meriweather Lewis and Captain William Clark, officers of the United States Army.

20. Sacajawea is married. Though Charbonneau had purchased Scajawea in accord with local custom, Lewis and Clark demanded that he marry her in a Christian ceremony. Sacajawea had never heard of such a thing but didn't object, and Captain Clark himself performed the ceremony. Charbonneau and his wife lived with the members of the expedition at Fort Mandan over the winter of 1804–05.

21. Sacajawea's son. During that winter Sacajawea gave birth to a son. His parents called him Baptiste, but the explorers nicknamed him "Pompey."

22. Spring arrives at Fort Mandan. In the spring of 1805 the expedition prepared to travel up the Missouri River to the north and west. Sacajawea was a valuable addition to the company, since she spoke the language of the Shoshone people through whose territory they would be passing, a land that was completely unknown to them.

23. Up the Missouri River by boat. The expedition traveled up the Missouri, passing through a world of mountains and canyons teeming with wild animals. Here we see the explorers sailing through a mountain gorge while overhead flies a wedge of snow-white trumpeter swans, which must have reminded Sacajawea of the wild Canada geese of her youth.

24. Portage of the Great Falls of the Missouri. The explorers had to drag their boats and supplies overland under a blazing sun to get around the Great Falls of the Missouri River, in present-day Montana. It took them two weeks of hard work before they were able to launch their boats into the river again.

25. The Bitterroot Mountains. Traveling through the Bitterroot Mountains of present-day Montana, the explorers suffered from the bitter cold. Sacajawea had to shelter her baby as best she could, wrapped in a Hudson's Bay blanket.

26. Sacajawea guides the expedition. As the expedition neared her old mountain homeland Sacajawea was able to guide the explorers. She remembered every trail and stream and hillside as if she had left only the day before.

27. Sacajawea comes home. At last Sacajawea came back to the beloved land of her youth, as she had always been sure she would. One joyful day she was able to introduce Lewis and Clark and the rest of the company to the Shoshone people, and to translate for her people the words of the white men.

28.   The parting. After many adventures the expedition reached the shores of the Pacific Ocean. Sacajawea at last saw the great body of water that she had heard the old Shoshone men speak of. On the return of the expedition to the village where they had first met, Sacajawea and her husband and son said goodbye to the company and watched them sail away. Little Baptiste waved the American flag that they had given him.

Later, Charbonneau left her, going off to act as guide to another expedition to the far west. Sacajawea, keeping a promise made to Captain Clark, took her son to St. Louis, where she enrolled him in school.

29. The last years. When her son was grown Sacajawea went for some years to live with the Comanche people in the Southwest, but she eventually returned to live with her Shoshone people on a reservation created for them in Wyoming. Sacajawea became a tribal elder, like the old ladies she remembered from her youth, passing on to the young her acquired wisdom and experience.

Sacajawea died in 1884, on the reservation at Wind River, Wyoming. There is a bronze tablet on her grave that reads:

Sacajawea, died April 9, 1884
A guide to the Lewis & Clark Expedition, 1805–1806